Everyday Life

Paul Dowswell

KT-157-849

Heinemann
LIBRARY

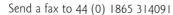 **www.heinemann.co.uk/library**

Visit our website to find out more information about Heinemann Library books.

To order:

 Phone 44 (0) 1865 888066

 Send a fax to 44 (0) 1865 314091

Visit the Heinemann Bookshop at www.heinemann.co.uk/library to browse our catalogue and order online.

First published in Great Britain by Heinemann Library, Halley Court, Jordan Hill, Oxford OX2 8EJ, a division of Reed Educational and Professional Publishing Ltd. Heinemann is a registered trademark of Reed Educational & Professional Publishing Limited.

OXFORD MELBOURNE AUCKLAND JOHANNESBURG BLANTYRE
GABORONE IBADAN PORTSMOUTH NH (USA) CHICAGO

© Reed Educational and Professional Publishing Ltd 2002
The moral right of the proprietor has been asserted.

All rights reserved. No part of this publication may be reproduced, stored in a retrieval system, or transmitted in any form or by any means, electronic, mechanical, photocopying, recording, or otherwise without either the prior written permission of the Publishers or a licence permitting restricted copying in the United Kingdom issued by the Copyright Licensing Agency Ltd, 90 Tottenham Court Road, London W1P 0LP.

Designed by Tinstar Design (www.tinstar.co.uk)
Illustrations by Martin Griffin
Originated by Ambassador Litho Ltd
Printed in Hong Kong/China

ISBN 0 431 13232 1 (hardback)   ISBN 0 431 13237 2 (paperback)
06 05 04 03 02   06 05 04 03 02
10 9 8 7 6 5 4 3 2   10 9 8 7 6 5 4 3 2 1

British Library Cataloguing in Publication Data
Dowswell, Paul
    Everyday life. – (Great Inventions)
    1. Inventions – History
    1. Title
    609

GLASGOW CITY COUNCIL LIBRARIES INFORMATION & LEARNING	
C003167478	
P	PETERS
28-Jan-03	£11.25
J609	

Acknowledgements
The Publishers would like to thank the following for permission to reproduce photographs:
AKG: p19; Corbis: pp4, 21, 28, 32, 35, 38, 41, 42; Culture Archive: p36; Food Features: p39; Mary Evans Picture Library: pp5, 20, 22, 25, 27, 33, E Andre-Sohn p8; Photodisc: pp29, 37; Science and Society: pp6, 11, 12, 14, 15, 16, 18, 24, 26; Science Photo Library: p43, NASA p31, Dr Jeremy Burgess p40

Cover photographs: DK/Paul Bricknell (l), Food Features (t), Corbis (b)

Every effort has been made to contact copyright holders of any material reproduced in this book. Any omissions will be rectified in subsequent printings if notice is given to the Publisher.

Any words appearing in the text in bold, **like this**, are explained in the Glossary.

C0031 67478

Contents

Introduction

This book looks at the kind of commonplace, everyday inventions we all take for granted. Some inventions are relatively new to the world – Post-it Notes, for example, have only been reminding us to buy another pint of milk, or ring our mums, for the last twenty years or so. But most everyday inventions have been around for a lot longer.

For example, many people who wander around the Roman town of Pompeii feel quite at home there. The town, which was covered and preserved by volcanic ash nearly 2000 years ago, is uncannily familiar. There are paved streets, drains, water supplies, council flats, parades of shops – even fast-food take-aways. These sold soup and bread, rather than burgers! It is easy to imagine that the everyday life of the average Roman citizen 2000 years ago was not really very different from ours.

The blazing lights of New York City. Electric lights had transformed the night-time appearance of cities, and the world had entered the 'electric age'.

How are we different?

But two great inventions separate us from the Ancient Romans – the **internal combustion engine** and electricity. The Romans would have been impressed with our roads and cars, but probably not that impressed. They built roads so well no one would do better for 2000 years. They had wagons and fast chariots, which did a similar job to a car. But electricity is another thing altogether. Electricity to the Romans would have seemed like the most eye-popping kind of sorcery.

Making life easy

A Roman slave would have looked with great envy at the workings of the washing machine. In those times, cleaning clothes was a long, back-breaking, tedious job. Today, we can do a week's washing by simply pushing a button. The ability of a microwave oven to turn a block of frozen food into a steaming, tasty meal in a few minutes would have made the Romans who manned the take-away soup shops sigh. Their day began with the laborious process of lighting a wood kitchen fire, which required constant vigilance to keep it going.

Of all the everyday items in this book, only seven do not depend on electricity to make them work. However, the lavatory, lock, Velcro strip, spray can, non-stick pan, ballpoint pen and Post-it Note all make use of electricity in their manufacture.

Fear of the unknown

The arrival of electrical power in the 19th century led to a whole flurry of life-changing inventions in one incredible 100-year period between 1850 and 1950. In the early 20th century, however, when electricity first began to be installed in offices and homes, there was a widespread fear of it. The first electric lights were usually accompanied by a notice that said, 'The use of electricity for lighting is in no way detrimental to health, nor does it affect the soundness of sleep.' People knew electricity could be fatal – the electric chair (first used in 1888) made this plain enough. But many people worried that electricity would seep out from the mains at night, like a deadly gas, and kill them. Today, a hundred years later, we take it for granted. It is impossible to imagine a world without electricity and the thousands of everyday items that depend on it.

A collection of electrical goods from the mid-1920s. At first only wealthy homes had an electricity supply installed, but by the 1950s the electric toaster, kettle and fire you can see here were commonplace in most households.

Lock, 2000BC

It may be unoriginal to say 'there's nothing new under the sun', but in the case of the Yale lock, it's absolutely true. In 1848 the American, Linus Yale, secured the fortune of his lock manufacturing company with the 'pin-tumbler cylinder lock' – the first lock to use a small, flat key. He used a mechanism remarkably similar to that of the first locks, which are thought to have been invented in Egypt about 4000 years ago. They were built of wood and had a complicated arrangement of bars and pins that could be lined up with a key. Once in line, a bolt could be slid back to allow a door to open.

Bramah's 'unpickable' lock convinced many a buyer that they were safe with his products. The lock was eventually opened by an American locksmith named AC Hobbs in 1851. Hobbs took 16 days to pick it!

Ancient locks

The Ancient Greeks had locks, too, but these were more primitive and could be easily 'picked' with a stick. Ancient Roman locks were much more sophisticated. They were made of iron and had intricate bronze keys to open them, often fashioned in animal shapes. The Romans even invented the padlock. Medieval locks were often beautifully ornate, but the mechanism in them would have presented no surprises to a Roman locksmith. Nothing really changed for 1500 years.

18th-century changes

In 1778 English locksmith Robert Barron invented the tumbler lock. This uses a key, which slides a metal tumbler attached to a bolt in and out of the door. Some locks of this type had several **levers** to make them more difficult to pick.

In 1784 English inventor Joseph Bramah came up with another new twist on the lock mechanism. His locks had complex tubular keys. They were so difficult to break into that Bramah even put one in his shop window with a notice saying he would give 200 guineas to anyone who could pick it. Bramah pioneered **mass-production** with his locks. Helped by a very talented toolmaker named Henry Maudslay, he designed factory machines that could turn out identical, **precision-engineered** parts for the locks' intricate mechanisms.

Spoilt for choice

Today, a bewildering number of locks are used in everyday life throughout the world. Magnetic locks, combination locks, electric locks and time locks use keys and combinations of numbers. Computer locks rely on codewords, and biometric locks 'recognize' an authorized person by a particular feature, such as their voice, fingerprints or even the iris in their eye. But the locks invented by Barron and Yale are still the most common found in people's homes.

Joseph Bramah (1748–1814)

As well as being a locksmith, English inventor Joseph Bramah made his name manufacturing lavatories. He also invented the **hydraulic** press, the fire engine, the beer pump and an early type of fountain pen. Bramah fell out with his colleague Henry Maudslay over a salary increase. Maudslay went on to become one of the most significant factory machine inventors in the world.

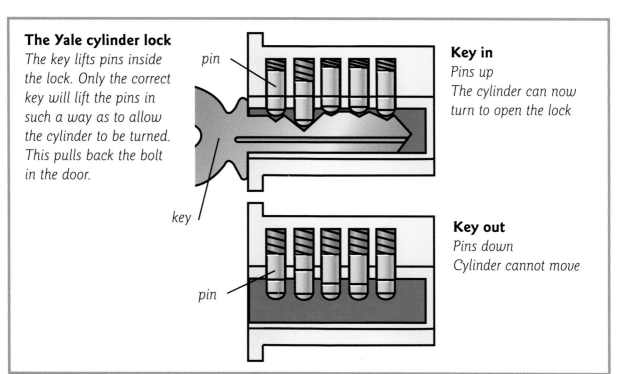

The Yale cylinder lock
The key lifts pins inside the lock. Only the correct key will lift the pins in such a way as to allow the cylinder to be turned. This pulls back the bolt in the door.

pin

key

pin

Key in
Pins up
The cylinder can now turn to open the lock

Key out
Pins down
Cylinder cannot move

2000BC	1778	1784	1848
ANCIENT EGYPTIANS ARE USING LOCKS	ROBERT BARRON INVENTS TUMBLER LOCK	JOSEPH BRAMAH INVENTS TUBULAR KEY AND LOCK MECHANISM, WHICH REMAINS UNPICKED FOR 67 YEARS	LINUS YALE INVENTS PIN-TUMBLER CYLINDER LOCK

Central heating, 150BC

Heat has been essential to people ever since the first cavemen began to move away from the warm African grasslands to colder climates in the north. Much of what we know about the life of the earliest humans comes from the remains of the wood fires they left on their travels. The first huts had fires in them, too, usually in a central pit. The fires provided warmth, light and heat for cooking.

The open fire was the main source of heat for thousands of years, until the Ancient Romans devised something better – central heating. This is an economical and efficient way of heating a building using one heat source rather than many.

The hypocaust

Roman home-builders constructed the first central heating systems in around 150BC. They used a single fire, placed in a shed on the outside of a building, which heated the air in a chamber under the floor. This warmed tiles on the floor above, which spread the heat evenly all over the building. The heat and smoke eventually escaped through vents in the side of the building. This form of central heating was called the hypocaust system, from two Greek words meaning 'the place heated from below'.

In 150BC most of the Roman Empire was made up of warm Mediterranean countries, and the hypocaust system was mainly used in public bathhouses. But as the Empire expanded into the colder climates of Northern Europe and Britain, central heating became increasingly necessary in the houses built by wealthy Romans in these territories.

Roman central heating was efficient and effective, and essential for villas in the Northern Empire, where winters were colder than those in Italy.

fire in outer building

Back to the old ways

With the fall of the Roman Empire in the 5th century AD, the wealthy Romans' villas and central heating systems fell into ruin. Most people had not been wealthy enough to live in such grand houses, and carried on warming themselves with the wood fires they had always used.

By the 17th century, people were burning so much wood on fires that governments worried there would not be enough available for building ships and houses. Instead, people began to use coal and other **fossil fuels** such as peat.

Central heating returns

It was not until the late 18th and early 19th centuries that the idea of central heating reappeared. At this time, factory owners realized that steam central heating would be a cheap and convenient method of heating their buildings. Central heating using hot water and radiators was installed in a few houses around this time. It was not until the first half of the 20th century, however, that houses began to have this kind of central heating on any widespread scale.

Today, householders can choose between gas, electricity, oil and solid fuels as the energy supply for their central heating system. Some people even use **solar power**. They can use hot water, steam or warm air to heat radiators, or underfloor and wall pipes. Warm air vents supplied from a central heat source are especially common in North America.

c. 150BC	c. AD 1800	1816	1835
HYPOCAUST CENTRAL HEATING INSTALLED IN ROMAN BUILDINGS	STEAM CENTRAL HEATING INSTALLED IN SOME FACTORIES IN ENGLAND	FIRST HOT WATER CENTRAL HEATING SYSTEM INSTALLED IN EUROPEAN HOME	FIRST WARM AIR CENTRAL HEATING SYSTEM INSTALLED IN EUROPEAN HOME

Mechanical clock, AD 1092

In a previous age, clocks were considered to be the most marvellous, intricate machines ever invented. Even today, the tiny screws, cogs, spindles and springs that make up the miniature mechanisms of ancient timepieces still inspire admiration for the skill and patience of the craftsmen who made them.

The first humans understood the passage of time by the position of the Sun in the sky. As civilizations developed, people soon realized that everything in the sky went back to the same place once every 365 days, or so.

Marking time

As time went by, devices were developed that could measure the passage of time during the day. Shadow clocks – sticks in the ground that cast a shadow – were developed in Ancient Egypt, and other civilizations, before 3000BC. Another early timekeeper found in cultures as far apart as China and North America was the water clock. This measured time by the level of the water as shown on notches in a slowly emptying or filling vessel. Other devices included candle clocks and sandglasses.

First clocks

The first mechanical clock we know of was invented by a Chinese monk called Su Sung in 1092. It was an intricate device, powered by a water-wheel. Mechanical clocks began to appear in monasteries and town centres in Europe in the 13th century. They were powered by a heavy weight on a rope. The pull of the rope moved a set of gears, which made up the clock mechanism. Most people could not read or understand numbers in medieval times, so clocks like these had no face. Instead, they chimed out the hours of the day. Dials were introduced in 1344, by an Italian clockmaker named Jacopo di Dondi. The first clocks with dials just had an hour hand. The minute hand was first added in 1577. The first clocks were large, unwieldy devices, and gained or lost as much as 15 minutes every day. In 1656, a Dutch astronomer named Christiaan Huygens added a **pendulum** to regulate the mechanism. Pendulums swing with a regular 'beat', and Huygen's clocks gained or lost only 15 seconds a day.

Later developments

The next major breakthrough in clock technology was the use of a coiled spring to power the mechanism. This was first invented around 1400 and finally perfected by the English watchmaker John Harrison in 1761. Weight- and pendulum-driven clocks were too heavy and fragile to be carried around. Spring-driven clocks were much smaller and more accurate, and would even tell the time on a storm-tossed ship at sea.

Quartz clocks, accurate to 0.0001 second a day, were invented by American William Morrison, in 1929. The vibrations of an electrically charged quartz crystal regulated the clocks' timekeeping. Today most clocks use this quartz mechanism. Since 1972 an atomic clock ten times more accurate than a quartz clock has kept international standard time throughout the world. It is maintained by the International Bureau of Weights and Measures (BIPM) in Sèvres, France.

A mantelpiece clock from 1680. As clock mechanisms grew smaller, clocks could be introduced into the home – for those who could afford them!

3000BC	AD 1092	1344	1656	1761	1929
FIRST SHADOW CLOCKS	FIRST MECHANICAL CLOCK INVENTED IN CHINA	DIAL INVENTED BY JACOPO DI DONDI	CHRISTIAAN HUYGENS ADDS PENDULUM TO CLOCK	JOHN HARRISON PERFECTS SPRING-DRIVEN CLOCK	WILLIAM MORRISON INVENTS QUARTZ CLOCK

Watch, 1500

Peter Henlein, a clockmaker from Nuremberg, Germany, is credited with making the first watch. His timepiece, made around 1500, was spring-driven, wound by a key and small enough to fit into a coat pocket. Like early clocks, it just had an hour hand, and it was even more unreliable. It gained or lost up to 30 minutes a day.

These early watches were carried in the pocket, or worn on a chain. The smaller they were, the more difficult it was to make the mechanism inside them. Watchmakers were among the most highly skilled craftsmen of their day.

Team production

Over the centuries demand for watches grew and production became more of a team effort. Perhaps as many as 30 craftsmen would be involved in making a single watch. By the 18th century watches often contained hard-wearing precious jewels, which were built into the parts of the mechanism most likely to wear out. Many watches also had a silver or gold casing. Not surprisingly, they were very expensive.

Wristwatches

By 1790 two watchmakers from Geneva in Switzerland, named Jacquet-Droz and Leschot, were making watches small enough to be worn on the wrist. By the mid-19th century wristwatches had become popular with women, because they were so lightweight and convenient. In Europe, though, men thought them rather effeminate.

A beautiful pocket watch from 1759. Its complicated, jewel-mounted mechanism was one of the finest technological achievements of its age.

This changed during the First World War when soldiers wore wristwatches in the trenches, for much the same reasons women had started wearing them 50 years before. By the 19th century, factory **mass-production** techniques were allowing watchmakers to sell their goods more cheaply. In 1892 American manufacturer Robert Ingersoll's wristwatches cost as little as a dollar, which was then around a day's pay.

Two-thousand dollar watch

In 1929 the **quartz** clock was invented (see page 11). This eventually led to the introduction of the first quartz-regulated **digital wristwatch** in 1971. Called the Pulsar, it was produced by the Time Computer Company of America, showed the time via **light-emitting diodes (LEDs)**, and cost $2000. Not only was it awesomely expensive, but the LEDs had to be switched on by pushing a button because they ran the battery down so quickly.

Despite this unpromising beginning, digital watches eventually took off in the late 1970s. Companies such as Timex and Seiko began manufacturing cheap quartz-driven digital watches, and the mechanical watch industry never recovered. Almost all wristwatches sold today have a quartz-driven mechanism.

Kinetic watches

Kinetic watches, also known as self-winding or automatic watches, were invented by an English watchmaker called John Harwood in 1923. They had a weight inside which swung around when the wearer moved his or her wrist. The weight wound up the spring that powered the watch, so the wearer never has to remember to wind it up.

1500	1790	1892	1923	1971
PETER HENLEIN MAKES FIRST WATCH	JACQUET-DROZ AND LESCHOT MAKE FIRST WRISTWATCH	ROBERT INGERSOLL PRODUCES THE ONE DOLLAR WRISTWATCH	FIRST KINETIC WATCH INVENTED BY JOHN HARWOOD	FIRST DIGITAL WATCH SOLD

Flush toilet, 1597

Disposing of human body waste became a problem the moment humans settled in towns and cities. Some early civilizations, such as the Minoans and the Assyrians, had sewage systems in their cities. The Minoans even had a form of flush toilet, which stored water from a stream to wash out a lavatory pan.

The Ancient Romans built brick-lined sewage systems. They were so well made that some are still used today. Roman lavatories were open-plan, and people sat around having a chat with their neighbours as they used them. A surviving one has 20 marble seats above a channel of running water. Roman towns and cities were well supplied with running water, which carried waste off to nearby rivers or the sea. But when the Roman Empire collapsed in AD 476, these systems fell into disrepair. The business of human waste disposal entered a dark and dismal age.

An illustration from Sir John Harington's book Metamorphosis of Ajax, *showing the workings of his Ajax flush toilet. He didn't really intend to have fish in the cistern – these are drawn here to show that his toilet uses clean water.*

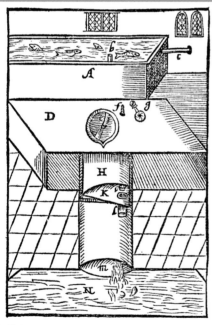

A. the Cesterne.
B. the little washer.
C. the wast pipe.
D. the seate boord.
E. the pipe that comes from the Cesterne.
F. the Screw.
G. the Scallop shell to cover it when it is shut downe. [53]
H. the stoole pot.
I. the stopple.
K. the current.
L. the sluce. [54]
M. N. the vault into which it falles: alwayes remember that (   ) [55] at noone and at night, emptie it and leave it halfe a foote deepe in fayre water. And this being well done, and orderly kept, your worst privie may be as sweet as your best chamber.

The Dark Ages

Monasteries were built with a 'necessarium' similar to the Roman lavatory. Castles had a 'garderobe' – a small extension on the outer wall, which hung over the moat. Some large houses had a 'house of easement' in the courtyard or basement. Cities had public privies – a wooden seat over a pit. But most people made do with chamber pots. People emptied these in communal cesspits, or simply threw the contents out of the window. This caused an appalling stench and a major health hazard.

One of Queen Elizabeth I's godchildren came up with the first modern flush toilet. In 1597 Sir John Harington invented the Ajax. This had a cistern that flushed water into a bowl when a handle was pulled. The water carried away waste to a nearby stream.

Harington's invention was slow to catch on – the water supply was too unreliable to guarantee a regular cistern-full. In 1775 Alexander Cumming invented the S-bend. This allowed a small amount of water to sit at the bottom of the toilet bowl, and prevented smells from the pipe behind the toilet from seeping into the house. In 1778 Joseph Bramah (see page 7) produced a flush toilet that used an overhead cistern. This was operated by pulling a chain, and gave a more powerful flush.

Pollution

Unfortunately, over the next hundred years these flush toilets made the problem of sewage disposal worse. Most drained into cesspools which were emptied infrequently, and often **polluted** the water supply, causing diseases. In the mid-19th century the modern water and sewage systems we know today were created. The arrival of constant running water and a reliable method of carrying away waste water meant that the flush toilet could now come into its own. In 1870 Thomas Twyford invented the 'washout closet', which is still in use today. In this, Cumming's S-bend ensured that there was always water in the pan, and a strong flush carried waste away efficiently.

The Victorians made huge improvements to their water and sewage systems, making it possible for the widespread introduction of flush toilets. This example dates from 1880.

2000BC	1597	1775	MID- TO LATE 19TH CENTURY	1870
EARLY FORM OF FLUSH TOILET INVENTED BY MINOANS	SIR JOHN HARINGTON INVENTS THE FIRST MODERN FLUSH TOILET	ALEXANDER CUMMING INVENTS THE S-BEND	BETTER WATER SUPPLY AND SEWAGE SYSTEMS PAVE WAY FOR WIDESPREAD INTRODUCTION OF FLUSH TOILETS	THOMAS TWYFORD INVENTS 'WASHOUT CLOSET' - THE DESIGN USED IN MOST TOILETS TODAY

Lawn mower, 1830

In the past, only the grandest houses had lawns. Servants with scythes kept them trim. But as suburbs grew up around the major cities of the 19th century, the European and American middle classes began to acquire their own lawns. They discovered that keeping them looking good was a major weekly chore.

British engineer Edwin Budding was mulling over this problem in 1830 as he worked in a textile mill. He noticed how the cutting machine he was tending trimmed the velvet fabric the factory produced. He wondered if such a device could be used to cut grass. Realizing he had had an idea that might make him money, he sought a business partner to help him exploit it. Teaming up with John Ferrabee, he produced a mower that is basically the same as the push-mowers used today. It had 46-centimetre (19-inch) cutting blades mounted on a **cylinder**. This was powered by a back roller which turned a series of **gears** linked to the cylinder as the mower was pushed forward to cut the grass. As the cylinder rotated, it deposited the cuttings in a tray at the front.

The world's first lawn mower, 1830. Edwin Budding and John Ferrabee's basic design has altered little over the last 170 years.

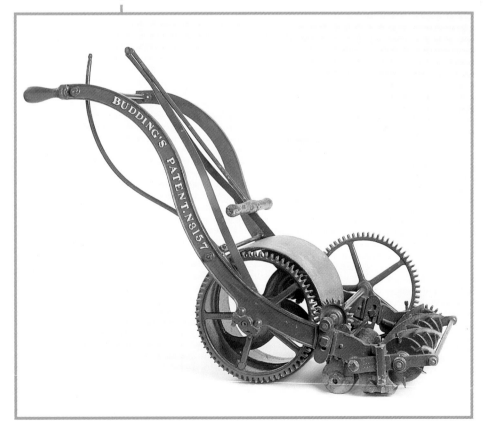

Budding and Ferrabee were shrewd enough to allow other companies to produce their invention under **licence**. They were well rewarded for inventing a machine that made it possible for anyone to have a well-kept lawn.

Mower power

As the century wore on, gardening became a major leisure activity. The first gardening magazine appeared in 1830, the same year that the lawn mower was invented. Whatever the advantages of the lawn mower, pushing one along was still hard work, and engineers were endlessly attempting to improve it. Horse-drawn mowers followed soon after the initial push-mower. The horses wore padded leather boots so their hooves would disturb the lawn as little as possible. Steam-powered lawn mowers were invented, too. The first one weighed a lawn-crushing two tonnes. The **internal combustion engine** was fitted to lawn mowers shortly after its invention in the 1880s, and electric mowers became available from 1926.

No wheels

The years after the Second World War saw another major expansion of the suburbs. The demand for even better and easier lawn mowers led to the creation of the hover mower. First sold in 1963, and still popular today, the Flymo (Flying mower) was invented by a Swede named Karl Dahlman. He made a device based on Christopher Cockerell's hovercraft. It had a rotating horizontal blade that was lifted above the lawn by a cushion of air.

Today, gardeners with really big lawns can do their grass cutting sitting on a small tractor-like mower. Enthusiasts even race these mowers. Robotic solar-powered mowers are also available. Despite the fact that manually operated cylinder mowers are much quieter and more environmentally friendly, petrol- and electric-powered mowers remain the most popular lawn trimmers to this day.

1830	1890s	1926	1963	1990s
EDWIN BUDDING INVENTS CYLINDER LAWN MOWER	PETROL-POWERED MOWERS INTRODUCED	ELECTRIC LAWN MOWERS AVAILABLE	FLYMO HOVER MOWER FIRST SOLD	ROBOTIC SOLAR POWER MOWER INVENTED

Refrigerator, 1834

People have long known that the best way of keeping food fresh is to keep it cold. Archaeological digs in the Ukraine have unearthed food pits dug into frozen ground, which date from prehistoric times.

The Ancient Greeks and Romans carried snow and ice from mountain tops to chill their food and drink. In more recent times, European stately homes and grand castles had an ice-house in a sheltered spot in their grounds, where food could be kept cool.

In the early 19th century ice-boxes became common in American homes and caught on in Europe during the rest of the century. These wooden chests were lined with an insulating material such as cork or asbestos and held blocks of slowly melting ice, which were delivered daily. The ice was imported from northern countries, which had an all-year-round supply. Ice-boxes worked relatively well, but they were messy and inconvenient.

A 19th-century ice-box, used to keep food cool. It relied on daily deliveries of blocks of ice, which slowly melted and had to be drained away.

A cooling gas

Jacob Perkins, an American living in London, invented the first refrigerator in 1834. Scientists understood that people and animals keep cool by sweating. Water **evaporates** from their body, carrying heat with it. A damp cloth keeps a bottle of liquid cool in the same way. As water gradually evaporates from the cloth, it carries heat away from the bottle.

Perkins adopted an idea previously discovered by William Cullen, a chemistry lecturer from Glasgow University. Cullen had noticed that evaporating nitrous ether was particularly good at producing freezing temperatures. Perkins devised a machine that fed this liquid through a series of pipes. It is considered to be the first refrigerator.

Refrigerated ships

Nothing more came of Perkins' refrigerator until the idea was taken up by a Frenchman, Charles Tellier. He devised a refrigeration device for cargo ships in 1868. The world's first refrigerated cargo ship, *Le Frigorifique*, was launched in 1877. Ships such as this transformed the meat trade. It meant that farmers in Argentina and Australia, for example, could now sell their beef and lamb in Europe and North America.

In the early 20th century fridges began to be sold to ordinary homes. The first one, the Dolmelre, was designed by Fred W Wolf in Chicago in 1913. By the 1930s fridges were a common sight in American homes. Most households in Europe had them by the 1960s. Having chilled and frozen food in the house cut out the need for a daily shopping expedition, but the popularity of the fridge killed off the local grocery business in many communities. It also meant that people ate less healthy fresh food in favour of frozen or chilled convenience food – a type of product that arrived as a direct consequence of the invention of the fridge.

An American 'Coldspot Super Six' fridge from the 1930s. This fridge took its curved, 'streamlined' design from the motor industry, which had pioneered techniques in metal shaping.

PREHISTORIC TIMES	1834	1868	1877	1913
PEOPLE USE DEEP PITS IN FROZEN GROUND TO STORE FOOD	JACOB PERKINS BUILDS FIRST REFRIGERATOR DEVICE	CHARLES TELLIER DESIGNS REFRIGERATOR FOR USE ON A SHIP	*LE FRIGORIFIQUE* – FIRST REFRIGERATED SHIP – LAUNCHED	THE DOLMELRE, THE FIRST HOUSEHOLD FRIDGE, GOES ON SALE IN THE USA

Light bulb, 1848

The light bulb is a very simple idea. It uses an **electric current** to heat up a thin wire, known as a filament. The filament glows, giving off light. Its invention, however, is a long and tortuous story. It began in 1801, when British chemist Humphry Davy showed that light could be made by heating strips of platinum with an electric current. The strips burned up too quickly for the invention to have any practical use. In 1848 another British scientist, Joseph Swan used baked strips of paper soaked in tar and treacle to make filaments. Then he enclosed them in a glass bulb with a **vacuum**. This was essential because the lack of air stopped the heated filaments from bursting into flames. Swan had invented the first light bulb.

An American rival

Swan **patented** his idea in 1860, but did not demonstrate it to fellow scientists until 1879. By then he had a serious rival – famous American inventor Thomas Edison. Edison had carried out 1200 experiments in his search for the perfect filament. He had settled on **carbonized** bamboo, which glowed continuously for 150 hours when it was first tried out in 1879. By 1880 he had improved his design, and the filament could now burn for a whole 1100 hours (nearly 46 days).

Electric light illuminates a living room in 1885. Electric light gradually replaced gas lighting, as it was cleaner and safer.

Swan may have been the first man to invent the light bulb as we know it today, but Edison made massive improvements to the whole technology of electric power. In 1880 the first lighting system was installed, in the steamship *Columbia*. In 1881 a printing company in New York called Hinds and Ketcham installed electric lighting.

Thomas Edison (1847–1931)

Born in Milan, Ohio, Thomas Edison began his career as a railroad newsboy but went on to become America's most famous inventor. As well as the light bulb, he invented the phonograph (the first sound reproduction machine) and motion picture equipment. He also held patents for over a thousand other inventions. He set up a famous 'Inventions Factory' at Menlo Park in New Jersey.

In England that same year, Swan illuminated the Houses of Parliament with his own electric lighting, and the town of Godalming installed electric lighting in its streets. In 1882 Edison built an experimental steam-powered **generator** at Holborn Viaduct in London. Then he opened New York's first power station, in Pearl Street, Manhattan.

Partnership

At first Swan sued Edison, as he considered Edison's light bulb to be a breach of his patent. But the two men settled out of court. They set up a joint business in 1883, called the Edison and Swan United Electrical Company, to sell the light bulb in Europe. The basic design of the light bulb has changed little since then, although new metals for the filament, and argon and nitrogen gas instead of a vacuum, have been added to give a brighter light and longer life.

An Edison electric light advert from 1915. At first, many people were suspicious of electricity and thought it might seep out of the wall and harm them.

1801	1848	1879	1880	1882	1930s
HUMPHRY DAVY SHOWS HOW ELECTRICITY CAN BE USED TO PRODUCE LIGHT	JOSEPH SWAN INVENTS FILAMENT AND VACUUM LIGHT BULB	SWAN AND THOMAS EDISON BOTH DEMONSTRATE LIGHT BULBS FOR THE FIRST TIME	ELECTRIC LIGHT SYSTEM INSTALLED IN STEAMSHIP *COLUMBIA*	EDISON BUILDS POWER STATIONS IN LONDON AND NEW YORK	FLUORESCENT LIGHT TUBES INVENTED

21

Safety lift, 1852

Until the middle of the 19th century the tallest buildings were cathedrals. Two things stopped architects going higher. The first was their building materials. Bricks and stone are heavy, and require massive support for any building higher than ten floors. The second was that even if such buildings were constructed, the effort of getting up ten or more flights of stairs would make working and living in such places undesirable.

The building materials problem was solved in 1848 with the use of cast-iron and steel **girders** as a solid framework for a building. The stairs problem was solved five years later by Elisha Otis (1811–61) and his safety lift.

An Otis safety lift in use in the USA in 1877. Water was used to counter balance the passenger car.

Aiming high

Otis was an engineer in a bed factory, and he was asked to design a hoist to take goods from one floor to another. While working on this project, Otis wondered what could be done if the rope hauling the hoist snapped. He hit on the idea of installing spring-loaded **ratchets**, which would automatically grab the **guide rail** if the rope broke.

Realizing this was an idea he could make money from, Otis left his job to develop it. His big break came at a New York trade exhibition in 1854. Here he arranged for a hoist fitted with his invention to be erected inside the building. He stepped on the platform and had himself and several packing cases raised as high as a house. As a curious crowd looked on, Otis called for the rope holding the platform to be cut with an axe. The rope snapped, but instead of plunging alarmingly to the ground, the platform was held reassuringly in place by Otis's spring-loaded ratchets. His first lift was fitted in Haughwout & Co – a five-storey New York department store – in 1857. He went on to found the Otis Elevator Company, a name you can still see on many lifts today.

Improvements

Early lifts were powered by **hydraulics** or steam engines, but during the 1880s electric motors were introduced. Counterweights were first used in 1903. Connected to the lift cable, they go up and down the lift shaft in the opposite way to the lift, making the journey smoother and requiring less effort from the cable-winding engine. The introduction of electronic computing equipment from 1948 onwards made lift attendants redundant and allowed passengers to control the destination of their lift by simply pressing a button.

Today, super-tall buildings, such as the World Trade Center in New York, or Sears Tower in Chicago, have express lifts which zoom up and down at a breathless 500m (1640 feet) a minute or more. Like most lifts, they have sophisticated computer systems that control the order in which they answer calls. They also have touch-sensitive doors, which automatically stop the lift from moving if they are not fully closed.

How a lift works

A lift car is suspended by a cable that runs over a pulley at the top of the lift and down to a weight that balances the weight of the lift car and its passengers.

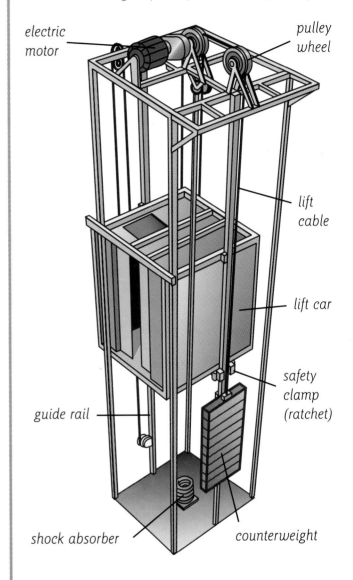

electric motor

pulley wheel

lift cable

lift car

safety clamp (ratchet)

guide rail

shock absorber

counterweight

1848	1852	1857	1880	1903	1948
IRON FRAMEWORK MAKES CONSTRUCTION OF TALLER BUILDINGS POSSIBLE	ELISHA OTIS INVENTS SAFETY LIFT	FIRST SAFETY LIFT INSTALLED IN NEW YORK DEPARTMENT STORE	FIRST ELECTRICAL LIFTS USED	COUNTERWEIGHT SYSTEM INVENTED	NEW COMPUTING SYSTEMS BEGIN TO MAKE LIFTS FULLY AUTOMATIC

Electric iron, 1882

Many inventions are ahead of their time, and one very good example of this is the electric iron. Invented in 1882 by New Yorker Henry Seely, it was a major improvement on what had come before. But at that time, only a few wealthy households had electricity, supplied by their own private **generator**. It took a good 40 years before most houses were connected to mains electricity and people could enjoy the convenience of Seely's electric iron.

Ironing long ago

Ironing pre-electricity was an even more tedious chore than it is now. The first irons were introduced in Europe in the late 16th century. The Dutch prided themselves on elaborate designs, but most other countries made use of a plain iron fashioned by the local blacksmith.

A charcoal-burning iron from 1850. Such irons were effective, but could be very messy if smouldering charcoal spilled on to clothing.

There were two types of iron – a box iron and a sad iron. Box irons contained a heat source. This could be a lump of heated metal, or red-hot charcoal. Sad irons were shaped blocks of metal with a handle, which were heated on a fire. They were called 'sad' after the original medieval word meaning 'heavy'. Anyone ironing with a sad iron usually kept four on the go. Three would be heating up while the fourth was in use. Both types required some skill to use, as they could easily be too hot and leave an unpleasant brown singe on clothing.

Safety

In the 1850s gas-heated irons were invented, and were swiftly followed by irons heated by oil, paraffin and even petrol. When Seely marketed his iron, he played up the danger of all previous methods by calling it the 'electric safety iron'.

Houses with electricity had become more commonplace by the 1920s, and sales of electric irons rocketed. A **thermostatic** temperature control was introduced in 1936, which made ironing by electricity even more desirable. It was certainly more hygienic than judging the temperature of the iron by spitting on it, which was what people usually did before then!

Today's choice

In 1926 a New York dry-cleaning company began using a steam iron on its customers' clothes. But it was not until 1952 that steam irons were sold in the shops. Hoover introduced a model that had automatic temperature controls and an aluminium plate with grooves along it, to distribute the steam evenly on the clothes. The iron also had an automatic shut-off when it was placed upright. Steam irons were slow to catch on, but today they are the most popular type of iron, outselling ordinary electric irons by five to one.

A servant ironing in 1896. In many households the iron was plugged directly into the electric light, when wall plugs were not available.

How an electric iron works

When an electric current is passed through a metal strip (called an element) inside the iron, it heats it up. This strip is in direct contact with the metal plate at the base of the iron, so it heats that too.

1590s	1850s	1882	1952
FIRST IRONS USED IN EUROPE	GAS-HEATED IRONS INVENTED	HENRY SEELY INVENTS ELECTRIC SAFETY IRON	HOOVER INTRODUCE THE STEAM IRON

Vacuum cleaner, 1901

In 1901 British bridge engineer Hubert Booth was passing St Pancras Station in London when he noticed the insides of some passenger carriages being cleaned with a high-pressure air hose. The hose blew dust off the seats well enough, but this dust merely billowed into the air, and then settled again in the same place it came from.

Booth was convinced that the air hose should be sucking rather than blowing. To prove his point he placed a handkerchief on a dusty carpet and sucked. The handkerchief immediately picked up a mouth-shaped outline of dust and Booth was on his way to a fortune.

The Goblin

By 1902 he was making **vacuum** cleaners for his own British Vacuum Cleaner Company, which would soon become more famously known as Goblin. Initially these machines were mounted on a horse-drawn cart. They went from house to house with a long hose, cleaning out any residence whose owner was prepared to pay for their use.

The first vacuum cleaners were large, clumsy and expensive machines. This one dates from 1906.

Booth did not have a **monopoly** on vacuum cleaner design, however. Machines based on the same idea were being invented throughout Europe and North America. The first portable vacuum cleaner was produced in 1907, by a company in San Francisco called Chapman and Skinner.

The Hoover

The idea really took off in 1908 when a harness manufacturing company in Ohio called Hoover began selling its own portable vacuum cleaner. The machine was based on a design by James Spangler, a school caretaker who was allergic to dust. Spangler had invented a curious device made of a fan and a pillowcase mounted on a broomstick.

Hoover bought the rights, and its machines used an electric motor to turn a fan. This sucked air, and any dirt or dust, through a nozzle at the base of the cleaner and into a collection bag. They were so popular that people talked, and still do, about 'hoovering' rather than 'vacuuming'.

The Dyson

In 1913 the Swedish company Electrolux introduced a **cylinder** model with a hose. Vacuum cleaner design then stayed pretty much the same until the 1990s. In 1993 British inventor James Dyson came up with his own spin on the vacuum cleaner. His models had no bag to collect dust, and worked much more efficiently than the standard design. His vacuum cleaners are now the most popular in Europe. The Dyson Company has become the first British manufacturer to export household electrical goods to Japan.

James Dyson (b. 1947)

One of Britain's best-known inventors, James Dyson is also chairman of London's Design Museum. He originally trained as a furniture designer and has turned his invention skills to areas as varied as boats and wheelbarrows. His famous vacuum cleaner went through 5127 **prototypes** before it was ready to be manufactured.

By the 1920s, vacuum cleaners had become small enough to be portable and easy to use. This publicity photograph for the American Hoover Company depicts a vacuum cleaner with a light at the front to show up dust and dirt on the carpet.

1901	1902	1907	1908	1913	1993
HUBERT BOOTH INVENTS FIRST VACUUM CLEANER	BRITISH VACUUM CLEANER COMPANY MANUFACTURES FIRST VACUUM CLEANERS	CHAPMAN AND SKINNER COMPANY SELLS FIRST PORTABLE VACUUM CLEANER	HOOVER MANUFACTURES ITS FIRST VACUUM CLEANER	ELECTROLUX INTRODUCES CYLINDER AND HOSE STYLE	JAMES DYSON INVENTS BAGLESS VACUUM CLEANER

Washing machine, 1907

Do you think loading a washing machine and hanging up the laundry to dry is a tedious chore? It's lucky you were born in the late 20th century! Ancient Egyptian washerwomen had to pound their dirty clothes on riverside rocks, and used a salt called natron as a primitive **detergent**. Even a hundred years ago, in Victorian times, the weekly wash was a dreadful ordeal of pounding, rubbing, wringing and rinsing. It took an entire day, and left the housewife or servant landed with the task feeling exhausted. In many countries today this is still how the weekly wash gets done.

The first recognizable washing machines were made in the 1880s. They looked like big tubs and had a hand-operated **dolly** inside them. This moved the clothes around inside the tub, which had its own gas heater to boil the water. Wet clothes were then laboriously squeezed through the jaws of a rubber **mangle**, which was operated with a big handle.

This Thor washing machine was made in 1907. Using it entailed boiling water, lifting clothes in and out, rinsing them in separate water and then running them through a mangle to wring the water out.

Step forward

As the 20th century dawned, electricity was beginning to be introduced into people's homes. Washing machines with electric motors to power their dollies and wringers became available. The first one was produced in America in 1907, and was called the Thor. It was designed by Alva J Fisher and manufactured by the Hurley Machine Corporation of Chicago. This machine was found only in the homes of the rich. It was very expensive and very unreliable.

Servant problem

Until the First World War (1914–18), many households in Europe and the US had servants who did their washing. During the war and after, many servants could get better-paid work in factories. A shortage of servants led manufacturers to invest heavily in producing a better washing machine for the middle-class housewife, who was now having to do her own laundry. At this time motor cars were becoming tremendously popular, and were being made in their millions. Washing machine companies borrowed from this new manufacturing technology. They were soon producing elegant, reliable and affordable machines.

Common sight

In the years between the two world wars (1918–39), washing machines became a common sight in American homes. In the United Kingdom, the machines only became widely affordable in the 1950s. By 1960 over two-thirds of all British families had one.

Today's washing machines are unrecognizable next to their ungainly, **predecessors**. Some machines even dry their load as well as wash it. **Microchip** technology allows a user to programme a suitable washing cycle for everything from silk scarves to **terylene** trousers.

This modern washer takes little over an hour to do work that would previously have taken all day.

1880s	1907	1927	1957	1960s	1978
FIRST TUB-STYLE HAND-OPERATED WASHING MACHINES	'THOR' – THE FIRST ELECTRIC WASHING MACHINE	HURLEY WASHING MACHINE COMPANY OF CHICAGO PRODUCES AGITATOR MACHINE – THE FORERUNNER OF ALL SINGLE AND TWIN-TUB MACHINES TODAY.	FIRST TWIN-TUB MACHINE	FIRST AUTOMATIC WASHING MACHINES	FIRST MICROCHIP PROGRAMMES INTRODUCED

Spray can, 1926

Science can be a double-edged sword. Cars are one of the most useful inventions of recent times. However, they are powered by **internal combustion engines** that have caused terrible **pollution**. The spray can is very much a mixed blessing too.

Spray cans are handy-sized containers filled with a huge variety of different substances and a high-pressure gas, known as a propellant. When the button at the top of the can is pressed, the gas squirts out the substance inside in the form of a spray, or **aerosol**. Spray cans have endless uses, from deodorants to furniture polish, from local anaesthetic to dairy cream. But their popularity has contributed to one of the most dangerous **ecological** disasters of recent times.

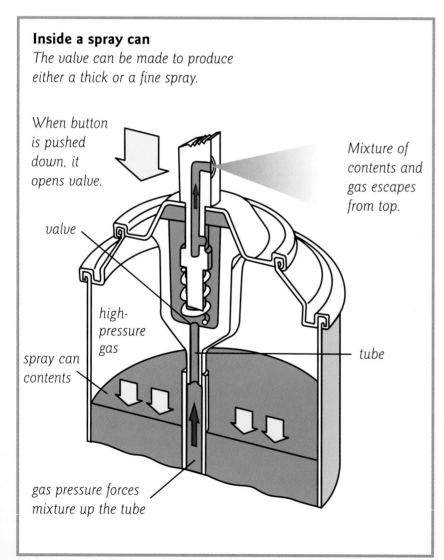

Inside a spray can
The valve can be made to produce either a thick or a fine spray.

When button is pushed down, it opens valve.

Mixture of contents and gas escapes from top.

valve

high-pressure gas

tube

spray can contents

gas pressure forces mixture up the tube

When people first discovered how to **pressurize** gas in the 18th century, they used this knowledge to make fizzy drinks. The idea of the spray can did not come about until 1926. In that year Norwegian engineer Erik Rotheim hit on the idea of placing a product in a can with high-pressure gas, and dispersing it in a spray, via a button and **valve** at the top of the can. This idea was taken up by two Norwegian manufacturers, Alf Bjerke and Frode Mortensen, who sold paint, polish and insecticide in these novel containers.

Bug bombs

The products were not a success, but the idea caught the attention of an American research chemist named L D Goodhue. He developed a successful spray for use against cockroaches. Goodhue's work was taken up by the American army during the Second World War, when soldiers fighting in the Pacific were seriously affected by disease-carrying insects. So-called 'bug bomb' spray cans proved to be a great success and were manufactured in their millions. In the years after the war, manufacturers began to sell a bewildering variety of aerosol products. By the 1990s, billions of spray cans were being sold every year.

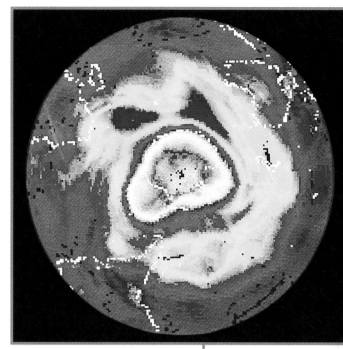

This satellite picture shows the hole in the ozone layer above Antarctica. It is shown here in white and pink. Most spray cans no longer use CFCs as a propellant, and the damage done to the ozone has been reduced.

Ecological disaster

The propellant gas used in spray cans was causing problems, however. From the 1950s to the 80s, the most popular propellant was chlorofluorocarbon (CFC). Once expelled from the can, it drifted into the upper atmosphere where sunlight turned it into chlorine gas. This in turn destroyed a layer of ozone gas in the upper atmosphere, which protects living things from the Sun's more harmful rays. Today, there is a large hole in the ozone layer above the Antarctic (where much of the CFC gas accumulated). The ozone layer throughout the world has been thinned, letting through more harmful rays. This has led to a higher rate of skin cancers and **cataracts**, which most scientists believe are caused by the rays. In the early 90s many nations agreed to use propellants other than CFCs in spray can manufacture.

1926	1942	1946	1974	1985	1990
ERIK ROTHEIM INVENTS AEROSOL CAN	US ARMY ISSUES 'BUG BOMB' SPRAY CANS TO PACIFIC TROOPS	COMMERCIAL MANUFACTURE OF SPRAY CANS BEGINS IN USA	SCIENTISTS MAKE PUBLIC THEIR FEARS OF OZONE LAYER DAMAGE CAUSED BY SPRAY CANS	DISCOVERY OF HOLE IN OZONE OVER ANTARCTICA	NINETY-THREE NATIONS PLEDGE TO PHASE OUT CFCs IN SPRAY CAN PRODUCTION

Pop-up toaster, 1926

Bread as we know it was invented by the Ancient Egyptians, who probably toasted it over an open fire. The Ancient Romans also sometimes toasted their bread. Our word 'toast' comes from the Old French and Latin words *toste* and *tostum*, meaning 'to burn'.

The arrival of electricity in western homes in the late 19th and early 20th centuries gave rise to a whole host of electrical goods for the kitchen and dining table. Among the new electric kettles, hot plates and cookers was the electric toaster – first manufactured in 1893 by a British Company called Crompton and Co. The toaster made use of **electric current**-resisting elements. These were metal wires which glowed red-hot when electricity was passed through them. The same idea had also been used in the newly developed electric fire and electric iron.

This electric toaster of 1910 did only one side of the bread at a time, and had to be watched very closely to prevent toast from burning.

These elements were placed in a small, enclosed, wire cage. Here they could glow in relative safety – either in the kitchen or directly on the dining table, where a breakfaster could toast away at will. Despite its obvious convenience, Crompton's toaster was tricky to use. It toasted one side of the bread at a time. It had to be watched very closely, to prevent toast from blackening, or even catching fire.

Popping up...

In 1918 an intricate toaster that turned the bread over came on the market. The biggest breakthrough in toast technology, however, came in 1926. Charles Strite, a mechanic from Minnesota grew tired of burning his toast, so he developed a pop-up toaster. This cut off the heat and popped up the toast when it had turned brown. It was first manufactured by McGraw Electric of Minneapolis in 1926.

THE "8-30" TOASTER

A highly efficient Toaster of exceptionally handsome design and beautifully finished in best quality Chrome Plate, it compares with many Toasters at much higher prices. It will toast 2 slices of bread simultaneously.

The broad flat top can be utilized for keeping warm a small muffin dish, etc.

Complete with 3-core Circular Braided Flex and Earthing Connector.

No.	Finish	Loading	Price
830	Chrome Plated	500 W.	**21/-**

...Everywhere

The invention of sliced bread in 1928 made toasting even more convenient. During the 1920s sales of toasters tripled, and the toaster became a household appliance as widespread as the electric kettle and electric iron. At the end of the 20th century, it was estimated that nine out of ten American homes had a toaster.

Today, the toaster has come to stand for a kind of cosy domesticity, and has often appeared in the work of modern artists. There are even Internet sites devoted to the toaster, such as Dr Toast's Amazing World of Toast billed as a one-stop source for toast recipes, toast haiku, toast information, toast links and toast gossip. You can find it on www.drtoast.com.

An early pop-up toaster. This 8-30 model, introduced in 1939, saved the busy breakfaster from having to wait around while their bread was toasting.

1893	1909	1926	1928
CROMPTON AND CO PRODUCE WORLD'S FIRST ELECTRIC TOASTER	GENERAL ELECTRIC SELL FIRST ELECTRIC TOASTER IN USA	CHARLES STRITE DEVELOPS POP-UP TOASTER, SOLD BY McGRAW ELECTRIC OF MINNEAPOLIS	INVENTION OF SLICED BREAD OF A STANDARD SIZE MAKES TOASTER EVEN MORE POPULAR

Teflon, 1938

Some inventions come completely out of the blue. One such is polytetrafluorethylene, known to scientists as PTFE, and the world at large as Teflon.

Teflon was invented by accident in 1938. Roy Plunkett was working for the Du Pont chemical company at its Jackson research laboratory in New Jersey, trying to find a non-toxic gas to use in refrigerators. One spring morning he and a colleague named Jack Rebok opened a cylinder of Freon 22. This was a **refrigerant** liquid which they had mixed with another chemical called peroxide, and then placed under high pressure to turn it into a gas. What they found in the **cylinder** was a white powder.

Wonder material

Tests on this substance, which Du Pont called Teflon, revealed that it possessed some extraordinary properties. It could withstand both high and low temperatures, and could not be **corroded** by almost all other chemicals. It did not carry electricity, and it was very, very slippery.

To prevent rival companies exploiting it, Du Pont kept its discovery top secret, although the American Military used it in its research into atomic weapons during the Second World War. Only in 1946, after the war ended, was the existence of Teflon made public.

Many uses

Teflon's slippery quality made it especially suitable for **industrial bearings**. Strengthened with graphite, or other hardening materials, Teflon bearings could be used in machines and engines with little need for **lubrication**. In medicine, Teflon's slipperiness made it perfect material for artificial ball joints. Because it was highly resistant to corrosion, it could also be used to make artificial heart **valves** and blood vessels. The electronics industry found it to be a perfect material for insulating electrical wiring.

Space technology was developing fast in the 1950s and 60s. Teflon was such a useful material for spacesuits and space rockets that many

people believed that it was actually developed by NASA scientists. One of its most useful qualities is its ability to withstand huge differences in temperature. This is especially important in space because spaceships and space-walking astronauts plunge from boiling to freezing temperatures as they go in and out of the Sun's rays on their orbit around the Earth.

Teflon's qualities make it an extremely useful material for buildings and bridges. The roof of the Millennium Dome in London is made of Teflon. The Statue of Liberty in New York has also been coated with it to make the statue more resistant to corrosion.

The Millennium Dome has roof tiles made of Teflon. Its strength, resistance to changes in temperature and fireproof qualities make it ideal as a building material.

Cook's help

The most famous use of Teflon is in non-stick pans. Curiously, Du Pont had not thought to use Teflon in this way. In 1954 a Frenchman named Marc Grégoire realized that Teflon's hard-wearing and heat-resistant qualities, combined with its extreme slipperiness, would make it perfect for pots and pans. In 1956 he set up a company called Tefal to make this kitchenware. Today it is still the most successful manufacturer of these products.

1938	1946	1956	1960s ONWARD	1999
TEFLON INVENTED BY ACCIDENT BY ROY PLUNKETT	DU PONT COMPANY ANNOUNCES EXISTENCE OF TEFLON	TEFAL COMPANY BEGINS SELLING TEFLON POTS AND PANS	TEFLON USED IN SPACESHIPS AND SPACESUITS	TEFLON TILES USED IN ROOF OF MILLENNIUM DOME, LONDON

Ballpoint pen, 1938

Ballpoint pens are so easy to use the French company Bic sells 14 million of them every day. Yet little more than a century ago writing with ink was a major inconvenience. Pens had steel nibs mounted on metal or wooden holders and had to be constantly dipped in ink every few words. The fountain pen as we know it was invented in 1884. It was a massive improvement on previous pens, but it leaked and still had to be refilled regularly.

An advert for one of the first ballpoint pens. Early models were expensive and built to last.

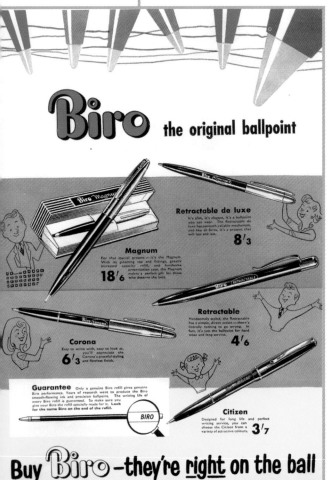

Buy **Biro** – they're <u>right</u> on the ball

The Biró brothers

In the 1930s a Hungarian magazine editor named Laszlo José Biró was pondering on improving his fountain pen. He hit on the idea of using oil-based printer's ink, which dries much faster than ordinary iron-based ink. He developed this idea with his brother Georg, who was a chemist. They tried printer's ink in a fountain pen, but found it clogged up the nib. So they devised a new kind of pen with a tiny ball-bearing 1mm in diameter at its tip, instead of a nib. The ball-bearing revolved around the tip as it drew ink across a page. It also pulled ink down a tiny tube from an inbuilt supply behind it. The idea worked brilliantly, and the Birós **patented** it in 1938. But before they could develop it, they had to flee Hungary when it was occupied by Nazi Germany in 1940.

Flying high

The Birós settled first in Paris and then in Argentina. Here they sold the rights to their invention to the British company H G Martin, who sold the first commercially available biros in 1945. The British government was especially keen to develop the ballpoint pen for aircrews, because unlike fountain pens they did not leak at high altitude.

The US government was keen on developing the ballpoint for this reason too, but the Biró brothers had forgotten to patent their invention in the USA. An American inventor named Miller Reynold produced his own version, which he called the Reynold Rocket pen. Marketed as 'the first pen to write underwater', it was an overnight sensation and famously sold 8000 on its first day in the shops.

Disposable pens

In the 1950s a French company named Bic began to sell its own version of the ballpoint. Unlike the biro or rocket which were expensive, used refills, and could be repaired, the bic was a cheap, throwaway pen. It was built to last, though – a fine-point bic pen could draw a line 3.5 km (2 miles) long before it ran out of ink. Its success was phenomenal, and by the 1990s the company was selling three billion pens a year. Despite the fact that ballpoints are smudgy, they are still the most popular pen in the world.

*The writing end of a ballpoint pen. The ball turns around like a ball-bearing, and uses the ink to **lubricate** its movement. Ballpoint pens usually have a ball made of steel or a tungsten-carbon compound, which is nearly as hard as diamond.*

1884	1938	1945	1953
FIRST MODERN FOUNTAIN PEN INTRODUCED	LASZLO JOSÉ AND GEORG BIRÓ INVENT FIRST BALLPOINT PEN	BIRO AND ROCKET BALLPOINT BOTH COMMERCIALLY AVAILABLE	BIC PRODUCES FIRST CHEAP, DISPOSABLE BALLPOINT

Microwave oven, 1946

Microwave ovens cook by directing **high frequency** radio waves called microwaves at food. Microwaves are similar to waves used by **radar** and are produced by a machine called a magnetron. They make molecules in food vibrate at an astonishing 2500 million times a second. This heats the food up rapidly and cooks it. Unlike a conventional oven, which cooks food from the outside first, gradually heating the inside, microwave ovens cook food inside and outside at the same time.

Researchers at the Westinghouse Electrical Company of Pittsburgh, USA, first discovered the heating properties of microwaves in 1932. They used a powerful radio wave **generator** to cook two sausages. Although they were impressed by the results, nothing more came of the experiment.

The magnetron

During the Second World War, British scientists John Randall and H A H Boot invented the magnetron, which was an essential part of radar equipment. Operators would test whether the magnetron was working by placing their hand near to it. If their fingers heated up, they knew it was working properly.

In 1946 an American engineer named Percy LeBaron Spencer was carrying out research on a radar-based project for the Raytheon Corporation. One day, Spencer noticed that a magnetron had melted a candy bar in his trouser pocket. He wondered if this device could be used to cook food. First he placed a bag of maize next to a magnetron and it promptly burst into popcorn. Then he directed waves from the magnetron at an egg in its shell. When the egg exploded in the face of a colleague who was peering at it, Spencer knew he was on to something.

The Radarange of 1947, the world's first microwave cooker. Like all microwave ovens it had a polished interior that helped to reflect microwaves back on to the food it was cooking.

High-speed chicken

Raytheon produced its first microwave oven in 1947. Aimed at the catering trade, it was called the Radarange and could cook a leg of chicken in an impressive two minutes and twenty seconds. Everything else about it was impressive, too. It stood 1.6 m (5 feet 6 inches) tall, and weighed a backbreaking 340 kg (750 pounds). It sold for a massive $5000 – around £46,000 in today's money. Unsurprisingly, sales were slow.

But the advantages of the microwave oven were too good to pass by. Further research and development produced smaller, cheaper and more efficient models. The first microwave oven aimed at ordinary households was manufactured by a Japanese electronics company called Tappan in 1952. Today, few homes in North America, Europe and the Far East do not have a microwave oven.

*A modern microwave oven uses sophisticated **microchip** technology to cook food to perfection. Many modern microwaves have an additional grill to brown foods such as chicken.*

Dangerous waves?

Many people wonder if microwave ovens are safe. The answer is yes, as long as they are used correctly. If food is cooked for a shorter time than necessary, bugs in it may not be killed off and may cause food poisoning. A badly fitting door on a microwave oven can allow microwaves to leak out and heat up the body tissue of anyone standing right next to the oven.

1932	1940	1946	1947	1952
WESTINGHOUSE ELECTRICAL COMPANY DISCOVERS HEATING PROPERTIES OF RADIO WAVES	JOHN RANDALL AND H A H BOOT INVENT THE MAGNETRON	PERCY LEBARON SPENCER USES MAGNETRON TO COOK FOOD	RAYTHEON PRODUCES FIRST MICROWAVE OVEN – THE RADARANGE	TAPPAN PRODUCES FIRST DOMESTIC MICROWAVE OVEN

Velcro, 1948

Fasteners have been around for almost as long as humans have been wearing clothes. The first were crude laces and wood or bone toggles held in place by leather loops. Buttons were first invented around 3000BC, but they were expensive and used more as ornaments rather than fasteners. In the 18th century factory production made them much cheaper. Zips arrived at the end of the 19th century. The first ones were expensive and jammed, but when they became cheaper and better after the First World War, they soon became universally popular. But zips can be fiddly and they do still jam from time to time. There was clearly room for improvement, and this came in the form of a fabric fastener called Velcro.

Hooks and loops

Invented by a Swiss electrical engineer named Georges de Mestral, Velcro was made of two strips of nylon, one containing tiny hooks and one containing tiny loops, which fasten together. Although they form a strong connection, they are easy to pull apart. It took a while for Velcro to become an everyday item, but now it can be found on many things, from shoes to sports bags.

A false-colour electron microscope view of Velcro. The pink loops are loose strands of nylon. The green hooks are thicker loops of nylon that have been cut in two. Each square centimetre of Velcro contains around 750 hooks and 12,500 loops.

De Mestral first got the idea for Velcro in 1948, when he was out hunting with his dog. He noticed how cocklebur seeds stuck to his coat and his dog, and wondered how they managed to do this. He looked at a cocklebur under a microscope and saw that it was made up of lots of tiny hooks. This was how the cockleburs had attached themselves to the looped fabric of his jacket. De Mestral realized that he had the makings of a new type of fastener.

Walking on the Moon

De Mestral called his fastener Velcro – after two French words *velours* (velvety fabric) and *crochet* (hook). Developing the fabric took over fifteen years, but when Velcro began to be produced commercially, it rapidly became a success. It was first used by aircraft manufacturers to attach insulating foam to the insides of their planes. American space agency NASA also used Velcro in its spacecraft. When Neil Armstrong and Buzz Aldrin walked on the Moon in 1969, they wore spacesuits which made plentiful use of this easy-to-fasten fabric. Velcro continues to be used on space clothing today. It is also used by space shuttle crews to attach their plates to trays, and their trays to tables, to stop their meals floating away as they eat.

In the 1970s Velcro began to have more everyday uses and started to replace laces, zips and buttons in clothing and bags. It is very long lasting and can be opened and closed thousands of times before its gripping power slackens.

Velcro is an ideal fastener for extreme conditions such as space exploration and mountain climbing. Here it is being used to fasten items to a surface.

3000BC	1896	1948	1957
FIRST BUTTONS INVENTED	WHITCOMB L. JUDSON INVENTS THE ZIP	GEORGES DE MESTRAL INVENTS VELCRO	VELCRO PRODUCED COMMERCIALLY

Post-it Notes, 1981

The Egyptians knew as long ago as 3000BC that boiling up bones, hooves and hides would make a glue strong enough to stick wood together to make furniture. Over the centuries people have devised a whole range of glues, and today synthetic (chemically produced) glues are more common than those made with animal ingredients. Glues are still used in furniture-making and other industries. They are also used around the house or office with such products as sellotape and magic tape. But one of the most popular uses of glue is the Post-it Note. Surprisingly, this seemingly indispensable aid was produced by mistake!

A useful mistake

In the late 1960s, in St Paul, Minnesota, a research chemist named Spencer Silver was working for the 3M company on its superglue product. During this research, Silver was attempting to produce an immensely powerful adhesive. Instead, in 1970, he produced a glue that was so weak it was considered to be useless.

Weak it may have been, but it was certainly interesting. Applied to any surface, it could be peeled off without leaving any sticky residue and then used again. This was because it was made of thousands of microscopic bubbles of urea formaldehyde resin, which contained an adhesive. These bubbles burst under fingertip pressure, but not all at once. This is what gave the glue its reusable quality. Silver spent years trying to find a useful application for his glue. Eventually, it was a colleague of his who came up with a winning idea. Product designer Arthur Fry sang in his local church choir. During every service he liked to mark the pages of his hymn book with slips of paper, so he could turn rapidly to the next hymn.

The humble Post-it Note – now an indispensable tool around the home, school and office.

But paper slips have a habit of falling out, and during one Sunday service Fry remembered Silver's supposedly useless glue. The next day he took some of this glue and attached it to paper slips. An extremely lucrative idea was born.

Sticky reminders

3M researchers spent the next year and a half trying to get the glue to stick to the note, but not the surface the note was attached to. The product eventually hit the shops in 1981. At first, Post-it Notes were sold as office stationery. They were used to leave telephone messages on desks or attach comments to documents. But their use soon spread to the home, and to schools and colleges, where the notes were found to be perfect bookmarkers – exactly as Arthur Fry had imagined they would be.

The glue in a Post-it Note looks like this under a microscope. The bubbles contain an adhesive that is only gradually released, as the note is reused.

All the first Post-it Notes were yellow – a colour which stands out, but is not too dark to write on. Today, they, and a host of imitators, are all shapes, colours and sizes. Post-it Notes are now sold all over the world, and people wonder what they ever did without them.

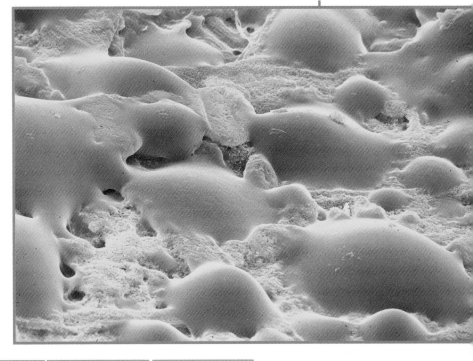

1970	1973	1977	1981
SPENCER SILVER INVENTS GLUE SO WEAK IT IS CONSIDERED USELESS	ARTHUR FRY HITS ON USE FOR SILVER'S GLUE	MARKET RESEARCH SHOWS PUBLIC INTEREST FOR POST-IT NOTE PRODUCT	POST-IT NOTES FIRST SOLD IN USA

Timeline

2000BC	Ancient Egyptians are using locks
c. 150BC	Ancient Romans install hypocaust central heating in buildings
AD 1092	First mechanical clock invented in China
1500	Peter Henlein makes first watch
1597	John Harington invents first modern flush toilet
1790	Jacquet-Droz and Leschot make first wristwatch
1801	Humphry Davy shows how electricity can be used to produce light
1816	First hot water central heating system installed in a European home
1821	Michael Faraday invents the electric motor
1830	Edwin Budding invents **cylinder** lawn mower
1834	Jacob Perkins builds first refrigerator device
1848	Joseph Swan invents light bulb
	Linus Yale invents pin-tumbler cylinder lock
1852	Elisha Otis invents safety lift
1879	Swan and Edison both demonstrate light bulbs for the first time

1882	Henry Seely invents electric safety iron
1893	Crompton & Co produces first electric toaster
1896	Whitcomb L Judson invents the zip
1901	Hubert Booth invents first vacuum cleaner
1907	First electric washing machine produced
1926	Erik Rotheim invents aerosol can
	Charles Strite develops electric pop-up toaster
1938	Teflon invented by accident by Roy Plunkett
	Laszlo José and Georg Biró invent ballpoint pen
1946	Percy LeBaron Spencer discovers microwaves can cook food
1947	Raytheon produces first microwave oven
1948	Georges de Mestral invents Velcro
1960s	First automatic washing machines
1981	Post-it Notes first sold in USA
1993	James Dyson invents bagless vacuum cleaner

Glossary

aerosol a liquid suspended in a misty gas

carbonized turned into carbon by heating

cataract an eye disease where the lens of the eye becomes cloudy

corrode to slowly eat away at, often said of chemical reactions on metal, such as rusting

cylinder a circular shaped container

detergent a substance that can be used to clean things such as clothes

digital wristwatch a watch that uses numbers to tell the time rather than hands and a dial

dolly a disc attached to a wooden shaft, used for stirring clothes in a bowl of water and detergent

ecological to do with ecology – the study of living things in relation to their environment

electric current the flow of electricity, for example, through a wire

evaporate to turn into a vapour and disappear into the air

flame-retardant a material which catches fire with great difficulty

fossil fuel fuels such as coal, gas, oil and peat, formed by plant or animal remains from prehistoric time

gears a series of different-sized, connected, toothed wheels, used to change the speed of a mechanism inside a machine

generator any device that changes one form of energy into another, especially a machine that makes electricity

girder a thick metal bar, used in construction of buildings and bridges

guide rail in this case, a long metal bar used to hold a lift in place

high frequency a form of wave energy, where the waves are very close together

hydraulic in this case, the use of liquid under high-pressure to move something

industrial bearings factory machine parts, which guide or hold other moving parts, and are subject to a great deal of wear and tear

internal combustion engine a device which uses a fuel such as burning petrol mixed with air, to power a machine or vehicle

kinetic relating to movement

lever a mechanical device used to transfer force from one part of a machine to another

licence in this case, a legal document giving permission for a manufacturing company to produce a particular invention

light-emitting diode an electrical device which gives off light

lubrication to apply oil or an oil-like substance in order to reduce friction

mangle rollers in a washing machine, used to squeeze water from clothes

mass-production manufacturing goods in huge numbers

microchip electronic circuits reduced to minute size and etched onto chips of silicon

monopoly the exclusive control of a particular product or service

patent an official document confirming ownership of a specific invention

pendulum in a clock, a swinging weight mounted at the bottom of a rod, used to regulate the clock mechanism

pollution the introduction into an environment of chemicals harmful to living things

precision-engineered made with microscopic accuracy

predecessor something which came before something else

pressurize in this case, to increase the amount of something, especially a gas or liquid, within a container

prototype the first version of a particular device

quartz a colourless mineral

radar a machine which uses high-frequency radio waves to detect the position of distant objects, such as ships and aircraft

ratchet device which uses a toothed wheel and lever to permit movement in one direction only

refrigerant liquid used in the mechanism of a refrigerator to cool its interior

solar-power power produced by heat from the Sun

terylene a light, crease-resistant fibre, made from chemicals

thermostatic reacting to heat

vacuum an area containing nothing at all, including air

valve in this case, a device that can be used to control the flow of a liquid or gas

Index

Titles in the *GREAT INVENTIONS* series include:

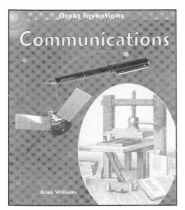

Hardback   0 431 13240 2

Hardback   0 431 13241 0

Hardback   0 431 13233 X

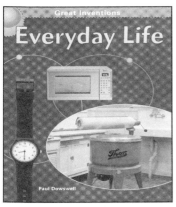

Hardback   0 431 13232 1

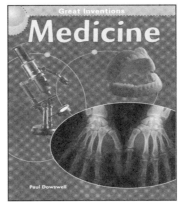

Hardback   0 431 13230 5

Hardback   0 431 13242 9

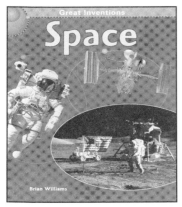

Hardback   0 431 13243 7

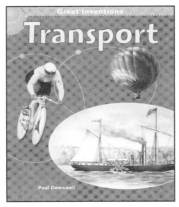

Hardback   0 431 13231 3

Find out about the other titles in this series on our website www.heinemann.co.uk/library